Dedicated to L & R.

Written and illustrated by
Paula Morales McDowell

@PaulaMoralesMcDowell

SOMETIMES I'M ROCKED

SOMETIMES
I'M NURSED

BUT I'M ALWAYS
LOVED TO SLEEP

Sometimes I get
cuddles

SOMETIMES
I GET KISSES

BUT I'M ALWAYS

LOVED TO SLEEP

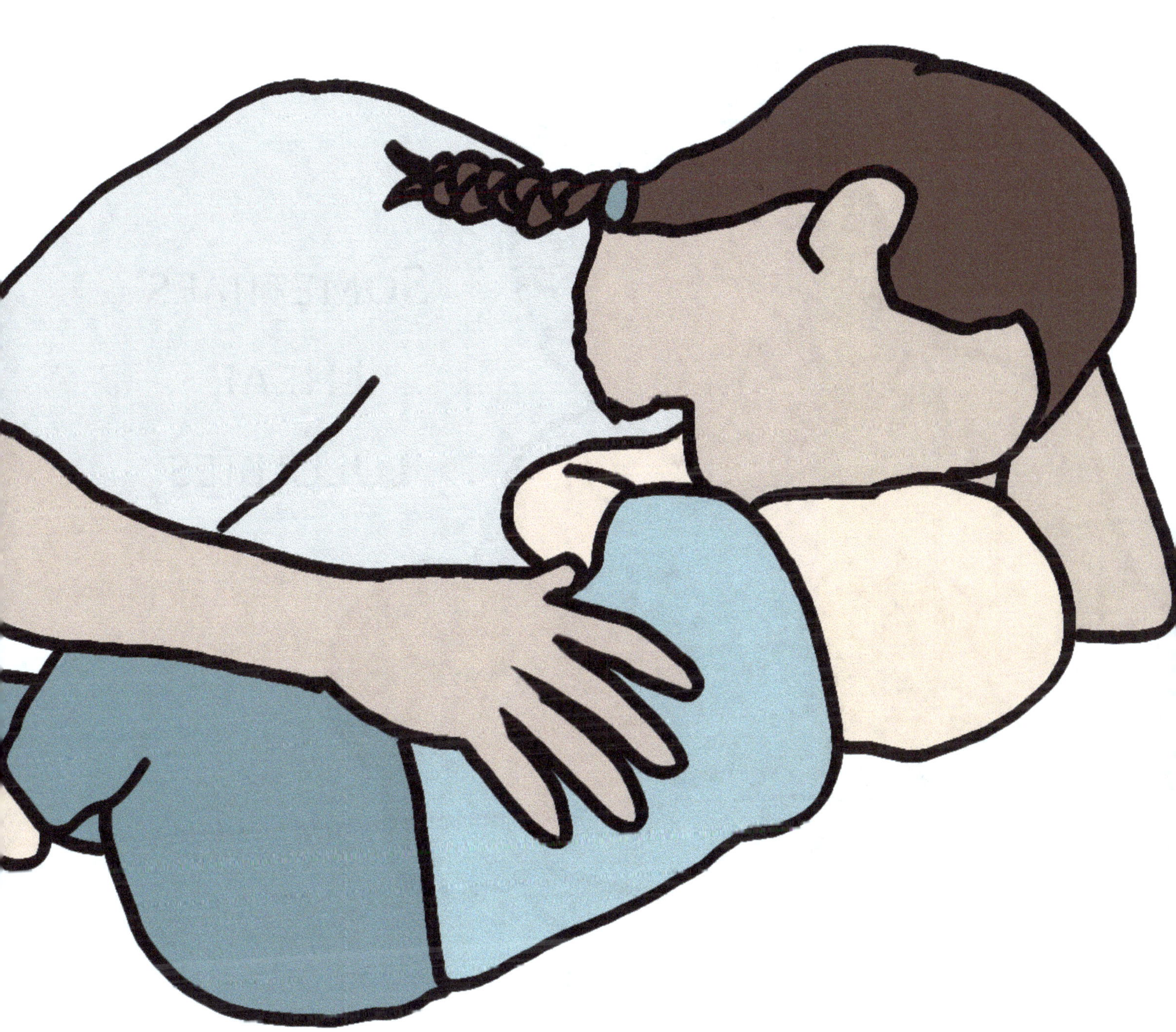

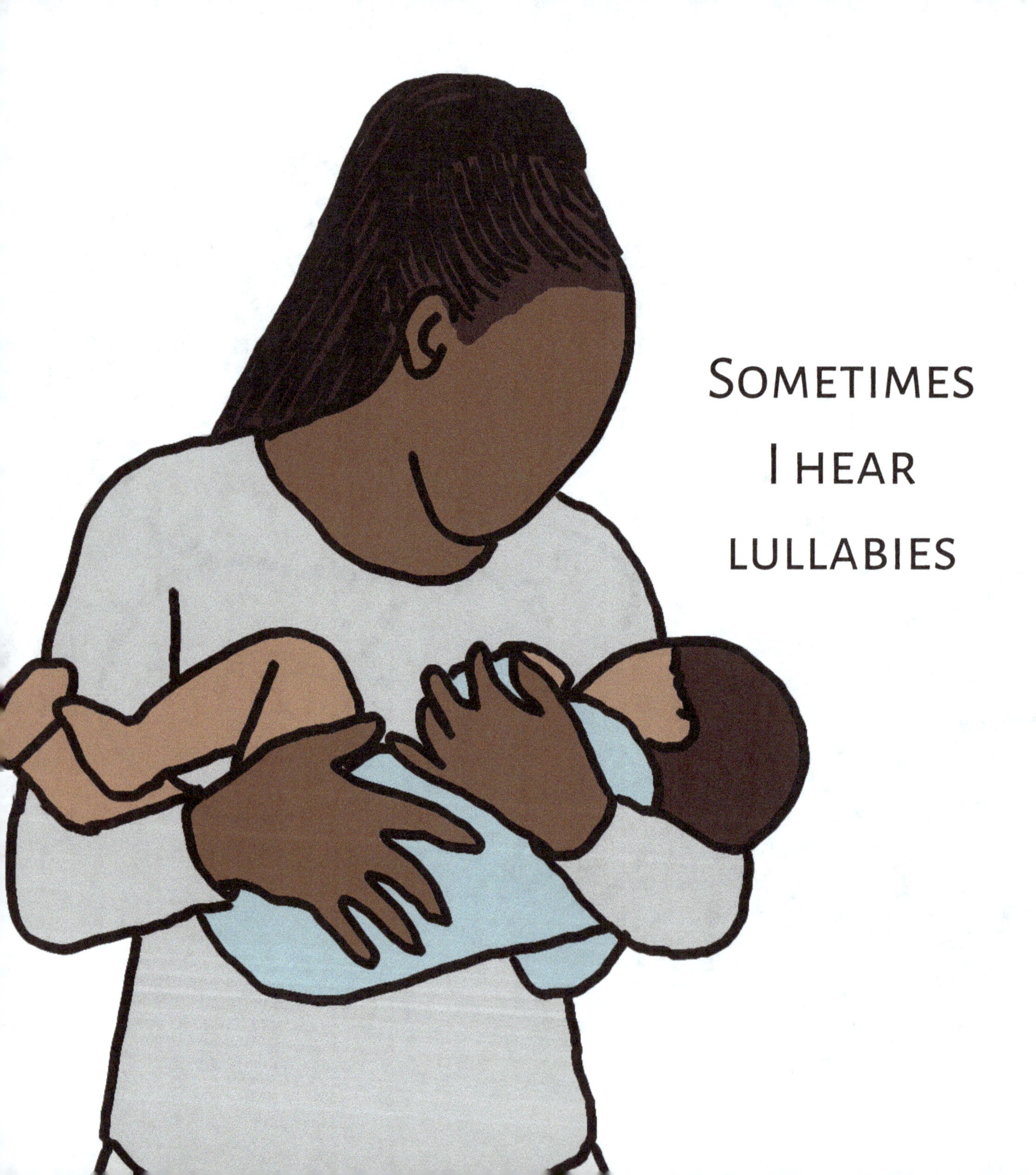

SOMETIMES
I HEAR
LULLABIES

SOMETIMES
I HEAR
STORIES

But I'm always loved to sleep

SOMETIMES
WE CHAT

SOMETIMES WE
JUST HANG

BUT I'M ALWAYS

LOVED TO SLEEP

Sometimes we hold hands

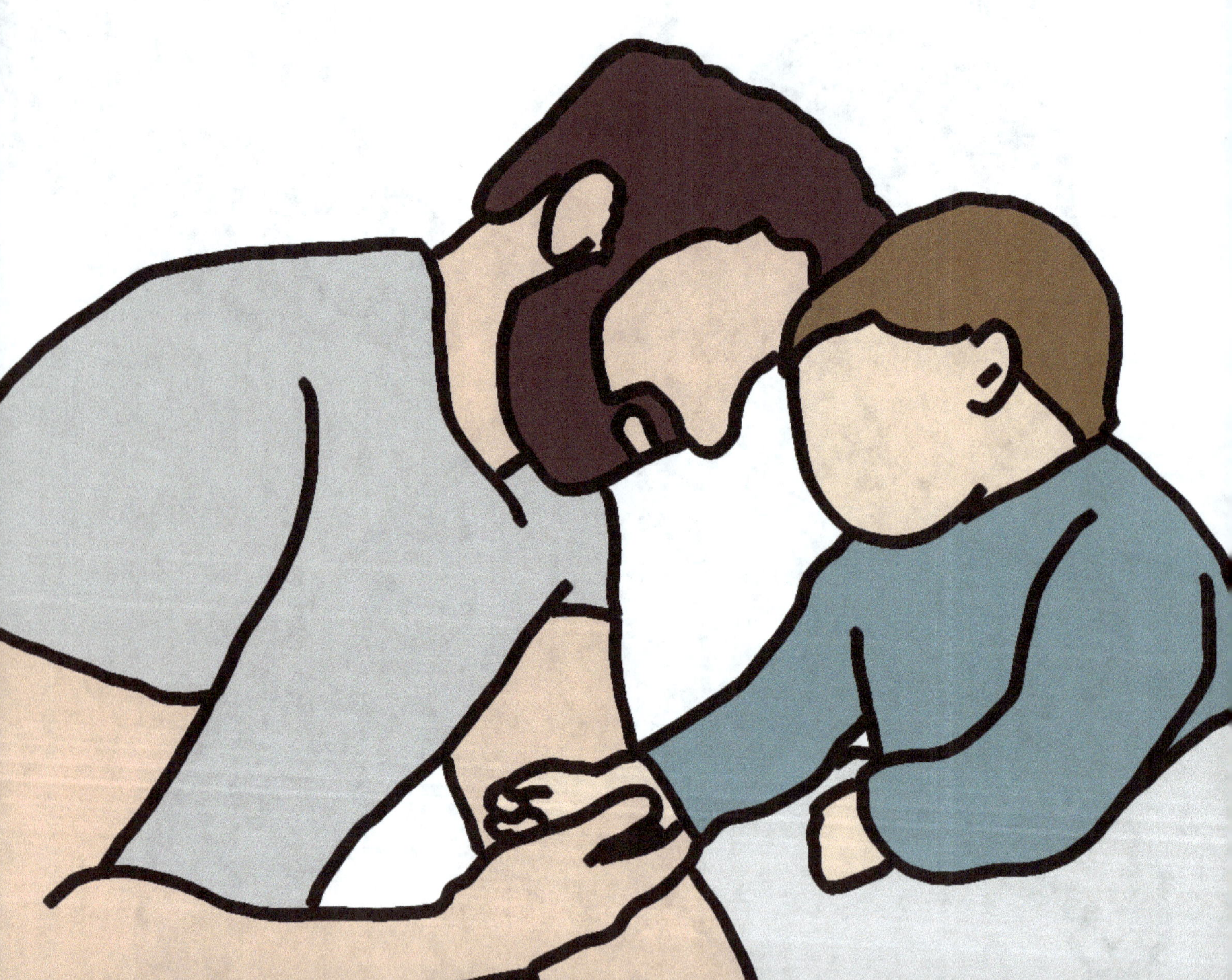

Sometimes
I hold my
bear

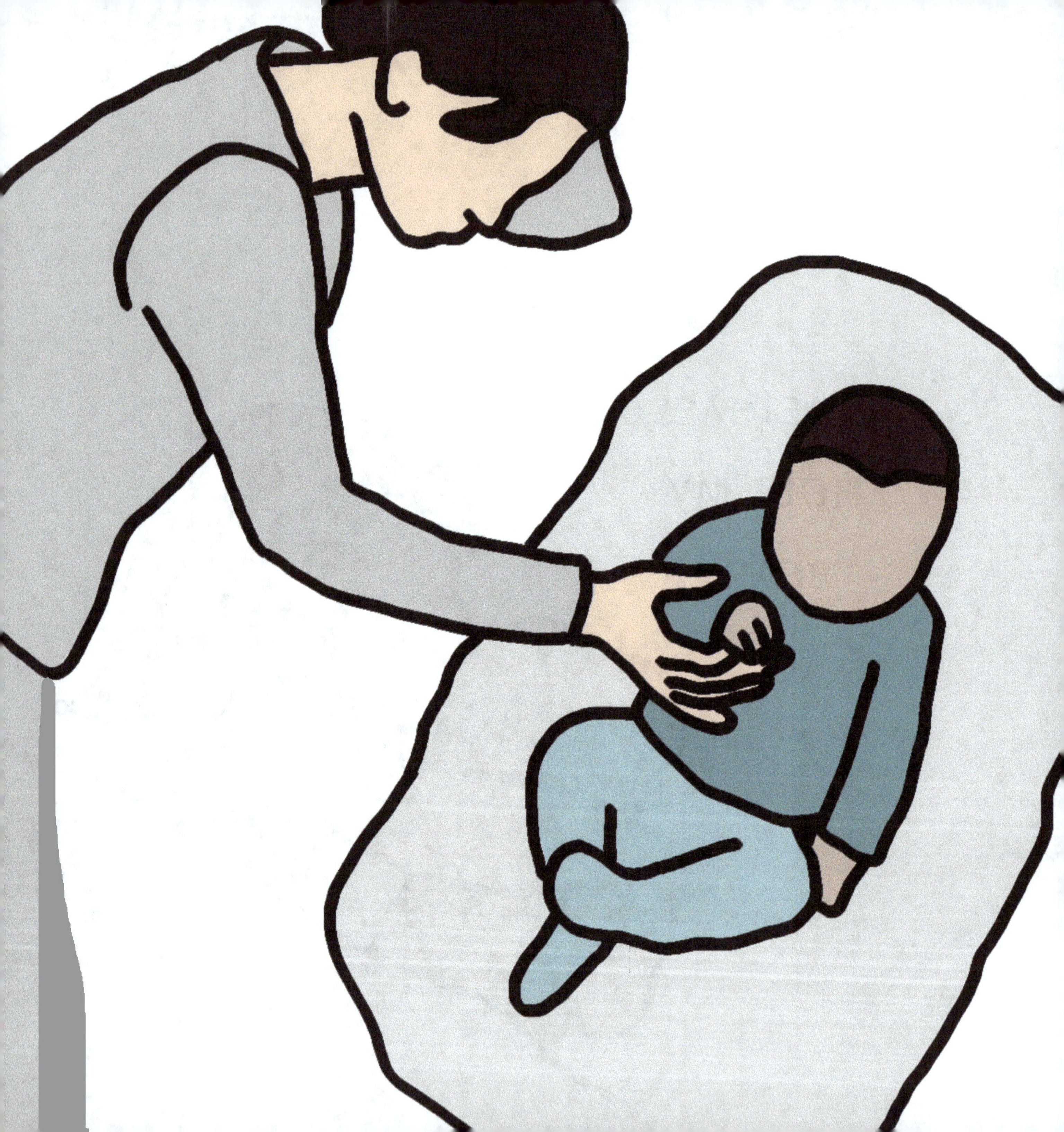

BUT I'M ALWAYS

LOVED TO SLEEP

I ALWAYS KNOW YOU'RE THERE FOR ME

I ALWAYS KNOW I'M SAFE

BECAUSE I'M ALWAYS

LOVED TO SLEEP.

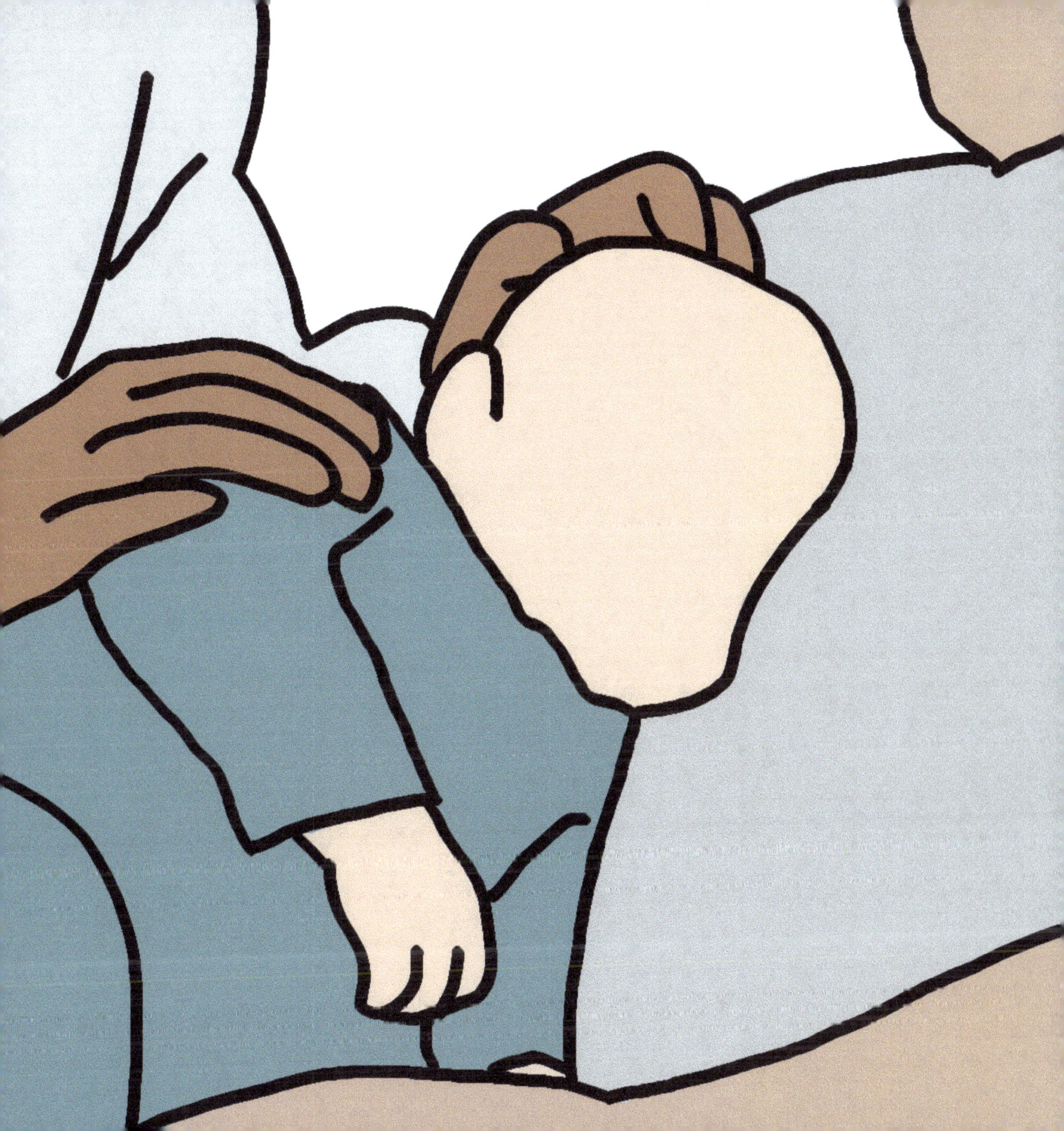